Fortune Cookies

Volume 10

Dr. Kareem Pottinger

YSD Publishing House

Library of Congress Catalog in Publication Data

Copyright 2007 by KAREEM POTTINGER

YSD PUBLISHING HOUSE
14490 Coastal Bay Circle 13204
Naples, FL. 34119

Library of Congress Catalog Card Number:
2013934185
International Standard Book Number 978-1-937171-09-4

Dedicated to my firstborn

YOUNGSABATH POTTINGER

If I ever leave this planet, I have
always kept you in mind.

Not leavening my wisdom far behind

Grow Good

INTRODUCTION

The true intent of this book
was to write a set of guidelines
that could be
immediately implemented in
the progress and advancement
of my sons elite
life.
This vast deep knowledge was
to be used as a
tool
to keep him far beyond just,
"ahead of the learning curb" for
lack of better expression.
These
rules are the widely accepted
and used unspoken
secrets amongst the elite in
which we use to rear our

young.
Although these are our
secrets
and most of us will and should
be extremely displeased for
having them on display for the
"normal's" of the world to
receive, I decided to release
them nevertheless.
For,
upon reading the finished
piece I realized that these elite
secrets
could not only serve to benefit
my son and family to come
well, but that the entire
world
could serve to benefit from
these lists of guidelines.
The way that this book is
intended to be received is to

ponder upon each page for a complete 24 hours.

Each page is to be pondered upon for the whole day; it is to be used as topic of discussion for that day amongst peers, friends, and family members' etcetera.

It is especially designed to be pondered upon mostly by you. For a complete 24 hours deep thought on each subject should be pondered upon. The reason being is to see how these guidelines could be implemented into your current life, how should they have been implemented in your past life, and how can they benefit your future.

It
is only through the true
belief
and usage of these
guidelines
that your life's
works will be greatly
affected
in its progress.

*In life
when it comes
down to
accomplishing
your goals,
there are
just
some things
that you
must
get
done*

In order to improve the outcome of certain situations in life, sometimes it is best for you to keep your mouth-shut

3

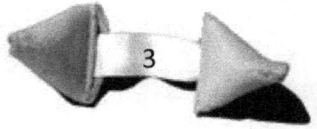

*Life
is
too
short
for
you
to
continue
compounding
your
mistakes*

4

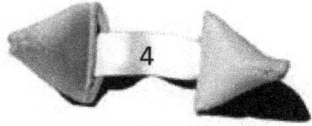

*Your attitude
does affect the
the
level
of
elevation
that
you will
accomplish in
anything that
are trying to
achieve*

5

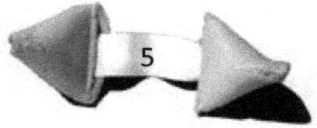

*The game in
which you
can not
see the
entire
playing-field
is
the game that
you need to be
extremely
careful about
playing*

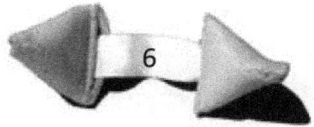

*In life it is
important to
understand
that not all
people can
be
mixed-up
with all people
because not
everyone
likes
all people*

*Small
steps
but
sure
steps
will
always
get
you
there*

*In dealing with
your romantic
relationships;
understanding
that love
will never
be able to
grow
under a
microscope
will improve
your odds*

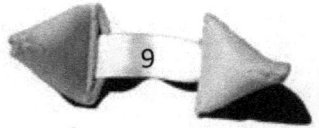

*When you have
experienced
how bad
things
can
become
you
truly know
what good is
when you are
in the
vicinity of it*

Don't get lazy after completing your task because the final finishing touches that you place on a completed-project absolutely affects the overall-value

*You have to
look at what is
best
for you down
the
road
because
that is what is
going to be
best
for you
overall*

*You
have to
learn
how
to
think
big
in
order
to
accomplish
big*

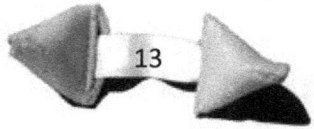

Depending
on
what
you
accomplish
today
is
what
you
will
become
tomorrow

Sometimes
a person's
eyes
are
forced
to see
more
than what
their
soul
can
handle

Nothing
worth
doing
will
ever
be
easy
to
complete

*You should not
be big on
issuing-out
trust but if you
are too, just
know that it
is a
virtue
that should be
earned
and
not given*

*The
more-work
you get
done
towards
your
goal
the
less-work
you will have
to do to
accomplish-it*

*You
should
always
place
your
smartest
effort
forward*

*There
are
no
reasons
that you
should
ever
rush
something
that
is important to
you*

You can not
expect people
to
support
you in
your
darkest-hour
but the
person
that does is
your
truest-friend

*Gambling
on
the
truth
is
not
a
gamble
at
all*

There are no rules on dreaming so if you are going to dream, make sure that you dream-big

*Good
connections
will
always
be
extremely
important
to
a
business*

*You
have to
chase
your
dream
so
that
you
can
catch
your
dream*

Sometimes
only
you;
can
leave
the
mark
that is
necessary
to
be
made

*After
every success
and
accomplished
goal
you
should gain
a better
understanding
of
your
abilities*

One way to insure that you will always be performing from your "top list of priorities" is to always remember that your time here on earth is not everlasting, and it does run-out

*You
don't
tell
people
with money;
what they
can do,
they
tell
you*

Always take a few steps at moving towards your goal while doing the best at what you can, while you can and your destiny will be revealed

*When
dealing
with
irate-people,
you
have to
stand your
ground
but
know when
to
back-off*

*The single most
important
relationship
that
you are
suppose
to
have in
this life is the
one
with
yourself*

*It is always
best
to proceed
with
what you
know
is happening
and not
with what you
think
is
happening*

*There are
two ways
of
making
money:
earning-it
is
one-way
and not
spending-it
is the
next-way*

When you
get-out
of
the
problem
and into
the
solution
your life will
instantly
become
better

In order for you to avoid confusion and focus-in on putting the best work out that you can, you should do one thing at a time

*In life; learning
how to
relax is an
aspect that you
will need to
retain
in
order
to
make it
to the
top*

*Calm
heads
are
the
ones
that
always
prevail*

*You
should never
miss business
opportunities
that can
allow you
to
achieve
advancements
in
your
life*

You
scarcely
get
baffled
when
your
always
paying
attention

*Although
principles do
stay the same,
be aware of the
fact
that the
applications
to
those
principles
may
change*

*No matter
how
great that
you
think
you are
there
will
always be
room
for
improvement*

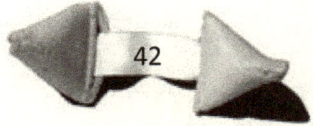

*When you learn
how to be the
best
in what you
do; it will
separate you
from
the
rest
and that in turn
will lead you to
greatness*

The faster you learn that the grind to the top is a slow-walk and not a quick-sprint, the less anxious and more poised you will become

*When
you
cannot find
what
they want,
you
have to
make
them
like
what you
find*

*Be wise enough
to realize that
there is always
a larger-truth
to your
immediate
agenda,
and that
larger truth
should be your
main
focal-point*

Your perception and the way in which you are being perceived will end-up steering the outcome of all your conditions

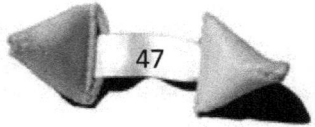

*You have to
lay the
ground-work
now
for the
progress
that
you
would like
in
the
future*

*When your
problems
are not solved
as soon as they
arise,
it is very
easy for you
to become
out-paced
by
those
problems*

The
proper-balance
and
proportion
is
vital
to
happiness
and
longevity
in
life

*Sometimes
it is necessary
for your things
to get
destroyed,
in order for
you to rebuild
them
back better and
even
stronger than
before*

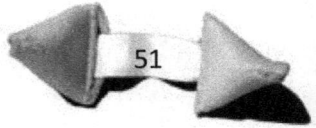

*Success
comes
from
the
universe
awarding
you
for
all
your
efforts*

*In anything
that
you
do,
you
have
to
leave
room
to
correct
era*

*Sometimes
you
need
to
remove
yourself,
in
order
to
improve
yourself*

The sooner you form exactly who you want to be in your brain, the faster you will become that person

*We as
human-beings
fall
so that
we
may
learn
how
to
pick
ourselves
back-up*

*Who you
think
and
believe
you
are
is
who
you
are
now
becoming*

*When
you
have
too
many
top
priorities,
you
have
no
top
priorities*

*It will
always
be
better
to
do
things
alone
than to do
them
with
bad-company*

*When you
do
less
to
accomplish
more,
it
increases
your
efficiency*

60

*Sometimes
the last
5%
that
you
put-into
a
thing
is
the
most
important*

When you are
too busy living
life;
you are not
actually
thinking about
the position
that you hold
and that is
when the proper
evaluation of
your true-worth
eludes you

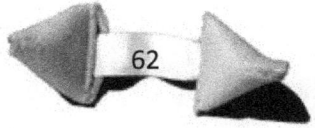

Goals
give your
life
a sense of
direction;
and when you
do not have a
course-plotted,
you will
end-up staying
in the
same-spot

The one thing that you must understand and never ever forget in your life is, no matter what, it will always be all on you, in the middle, the beginning, and the ending

Excess
in
all
things,
is
the
undoing
of
the
successful

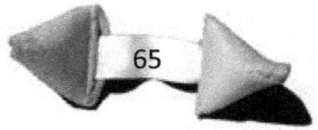

*It is
important
to
learn
the fact
that
you
cannot
invite
everyone
to
everything*

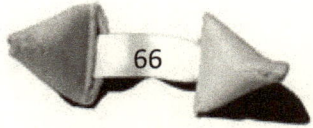

*No matter how
great your
appearance
seems
it will
mean
absolutely
nothing
if you cannot
deliver
the
package*

*All
things
are created
twice;
once in
the
blueprint
and
then
second
in the
construction*

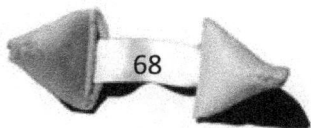

When your friends betray you, sometimes the only people that you can count-on are strangers

When
you learn
how
to
spend
less than
you
have,
you
will
always
have

*Sometimes
you
will
have
to
risk-it
all,
in
order
to
gain-it
all*

*Confusion
will
always
present
an
opportunity*

You should always want to finish your journey out on top; believe that you can finish your journey out on top and you will finish your journey out on top

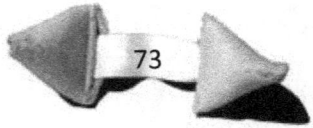

When picking a partner; it is important to pick someone who will push you to be your best and that will also compliment your aesthetic

*Confidence
can
take you
anywhere
that you
want to
go, especially
when
you
work hard
enough
at it*

*You are either
at the top
of
the food-chain
or
at the bottom;
there is no
middle,
don't ever be
fooled by
thinking that
there is a
middle*

*What you put
out in the
world
is
exactly
what you
will
receive in
return
from
the
world*

*Always think
about your
protection
and
health
in
whatever
it is
that you
choose
to
participate-in*

*Everything
that you do
adds-up,
all the things
that
you have ever
done
collectively
equals
you
at this
exact-moment*

*Your history
will
have a
way
of
repeating
itself
when
you
do not
learn
from it*

*In
your
life,
you
should
always
move
with
a
purpose*

*You can
accomplish
anything
that you want
in
life
if you
lack
the fear
of
accomplishing
it*

When dealing with money; all the relationships that you will ever acquire are truly just business and are not to be confused as friendships

*Real-love
and
understanding
means
never
having
to
prove
that
you
are
sorry*

Being
able
to
adapt
to
change
is
absolutely
necessary
in
obtaining
success

*Living in the
now
as much
as
possible
will
make
your
life
much
more
enjoyable*

86

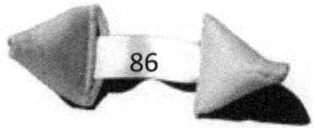

It is extremely
important
to
observe
all
your
options
be
for
making
your
next-move

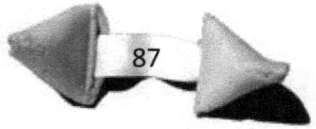

Sometimes
things
have
to appear to be
getting
worse for you
before
they
can ever
truly
get
better

*Your talent
will
never
mean
anything
when
you
are
making
the
wrong
decisions*

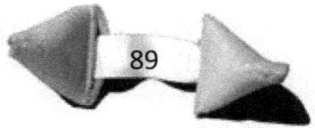

Sometimes
failing
is
what will
give
you
the
understanding
of
how
to
succeed

*Put
some
of
your
money
away
today
for
your
tomorrows*

*It is very
important
never
to
let your
anger
get in front
of you,
you must keep
it
behind you at
all-times*

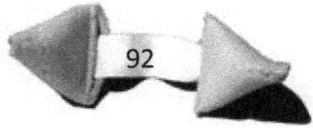

*Any
investment
of
yours,
you
must
always
protect*

93

*Your
safety
should
always
come
first
in
anything
that
you
do*

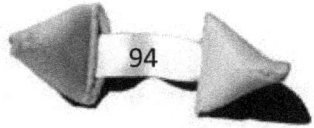

*One
of
the
keys
to
being
successful
is
networking*

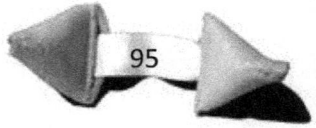

*When you get
rid-of
the
unnecessary
old,
it
will
make
space for
the
necessary
new*

*You could
never
truly-know
what
a
person's
real-intentions
are
until
it
is all
said and done*

*You have to be
patient
when
attempting
to move from
old
to
new
because it
takes a great
deal of
effort*

98

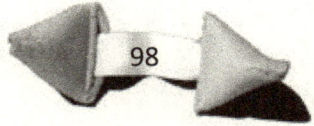

*There isn't
anything worse
in this world
than for the
outcome
of your
life
to end-up
to become,
that you have
done nothing
with-it*

*Your talk
will always be
just talk
until you decide
to put forth
effort
and
some sort
of
action
has begun to
take place*

*You
have to
learn
how to
let
things
happen
when
the
right
timing
unfolds*

*Just remember
that whenever
you
shake things
up,
there is a
potential
to
disturb
the people
that will
come after you*

*You
should
always
do
what
you
can
to
maximize
your
effect*

*In
life;
you
get
what
you
give*

*Don't
allow
yourself
to
screw-up
and
you
wont*

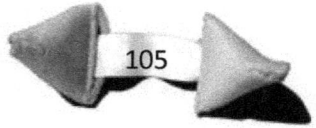

*Failure
is not such
a
terrible thing
when it is a
byproduct
of
putting forth
effort
in trying to
accomplish
something*

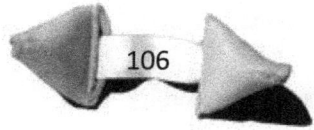

*The
forbidden-fruit
always
taste
the
sweetest
but
keep in mind
that it
is the
most
punishable*

It's important to evaluate your truth,
because more than likely your true-value is worth more than you are actually portraying

108

*It is important
to have dreams
and
goals in your
life
because they
take you
where
you
want
to
go*

Be wary of the
opinions
of
others because
they can
handicap
you
in the
pursuits
of
your
endeavors

*Be careful of
becoming
attached
to the
people
or
things
that have
already
served their
purpose in your
life*

*You cannot
out-run
the
destiny
that
you
have
set
in
motion
for
yourself*

*Don't
let
fear
sabotage
the
options
that
you
have
from
becoming
truly-happy*

*Understand the
fact
that listening
is a
choice
and you will
not be so
dismayed
when someone
chooses not to
listen to
you*

114

There
is
no-one
that can truly
stop
you
from
achieving
you
goals
but
yourself

The
actions
that
you
take
will
always
have
consequences

*Sometimes
in order
for
you
to
move
forward,
you
may
have to
go
backwards*

*Before you
make a
decision
you should
want
to know
how your
decisions
will
look
from every
angle*

*In
life
there
will
always
be
different-ways
to get
to
the
same
destination*

*Because your
time
here on earth
does not last
forever
and it does
run-out,
you should be
more aware of
how you should
be
spending-it*

*Experience
will
always
be
your
best
teacher*

*Life is too short
to be
concerned
with or to be
spending any
sort of time
with the
individuals
who you do not
like
or
appreciate*

When the money coming in can't keep up with the money going out; you begin to get into trouble, which is why it's so important not only to keep an eye on your finances but to keep up with them as well

*Any goal
that you set that
is worth
achieving; is
going to cost a
lot more than
thinking and
talking, amongst
the thinking and
talking it will
also
cost you work
and effort*

*Don't ever
let
someone
else's
opinion
steer
you
away
from
what
you
want*

*If
you
want to give
help,
stick with
giving help
to
the
people
who
can be
helped*

*In life
everybody gets
older
but not
everyone
shows
growth,
so have you
grown
or
are you just
getting older*

*It's important to
understand
the fact
that
great-things
can happen
from
your
mistakes
once
you have learnt
from them*

*Fake-friends
won't be able to
mask
their
true-feelings
for long,
so pay close
attention and
believe when
their
true-feelings
are unmasked*

*The power
that
anyone
has
over
you
is
the power
that
you
have
given them*

*There will
always
be
a lot
more
to it in
everything;
than what you
think you see or
than what
you think you
understand*

People will change only when they realize that they need too

*Sometimes there
are people
that are sitting
in the
front-row
of your life
that need to be
in the back, or
outside, or
maybe not even
evolved
in your life
at all*

In life;
sometimes it
will take
for you to take
the
wrong-road,
in order
for
you
to get to
the
right-one

*Don't forget to
weigh
all your
options
completely
and
carefully
as
you
make
your
decisions*

An
individual
knows what's
right for
them,
and
there
comes a time
when you meet
the right person
at the
right-time

*The
biggest
weakness
a
person can
have
is the doubt
that
they
carry
within
themselves*

*Continuing to
do just enough
to get
by;
leaves
you with no
room
for
advancement
in
your
future*

*When you
believe
in what you are
doing
and you are
putting forth the
proper-effort to
make it happen,
your
desired outcome
or even better
will be
established*

*You cannot wait
on
good-deals
all the time,
most of the time
you will have to
go out into the
world
and
make your
own
good-deals*

It is important to keep in mind that your results will always speak louder than your words

*Do not
let
your
emotions
ruin
your
opportunities*

*You becoming
out of
control
will
never
be a
good
place
for
you
to
be*

Sometimes
you
have to
accomplish
the
small
in order
to learn
how to
become
the
tall

*It is
up
to
you
to
think
bigger
so that
you
may
become
bigger*

One-step at a
time until
you are
on your
way
to the
top,
is all it
takes to
make it
to the
top

*Some people
will
always
remain
the same
because
they
cannot
accept the
fact
that times
change*

*Don't ever
forget
that
the
greatest-right
that you
have
is the
right
to
change
your mind*

When there is a
bad thing that
is happening to
you, it is
important for
you to
understand
that you
can always
make a
good thing
out of it

*You
cannot
become
great
when
you are
scared
to take a
risk,
fail,
or
fall*

*Some would
say;
to
not
take
the
risk
is
the
greatest-risk
of
all*

151

*You only
live once so
if you
regret
not doing
something that
you
wanted
to do,
then
that's
your fault*

*Always make
sure that when
you are making
decisions about
your life; that
the choices you
are
choosing
from are being
made from the
best of the
best*

153

*Your life
is one
big
continuous
work
in
progress,
which is why
you
should
never become
too content*

*Most times
all you
need to do
is
re-focus your
aim,
and the
outlook of your
life
will look
a lot more
promising*

*In life
sometimes
you
will reach a
plateau
in which you
must
fall-down
in order for you
to understand
how to get any
higher*

*You will make
a lot
less mistakes
in life
when you
learn how to
pace
yourself,
you cannot
take all the
steps at
one-time*

*In
order for you
to
achieve any
kind of success
in
anything,
you will
need to
execute
an
idea*

*Consequences
are
things that
hurt
but they also
can turn you
into a better
person
once
you have
learnt
from them*

The end

Additional books written by
Dr. Kareem Pottinger available online at

www.FORTUNECOOKIES.me

and your local book stores nationwide

<u>FORTUNE COOKIES VOLUMES 1-11</u>

also

available

on

your

<u>Kindle</u>

<u>Nook</u>

<u>Apple</u>

<u>devices</u>

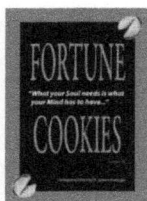

www.ingramcontent.com/pod-product-compliance
Lightning Source LLC
Chambersburg PA
CBHW030104070426
42448CB00037B/963